Building a Woman

Deborah Meltvedt

A Publication of The Poetry Box®

Poems ©2021 Deborah Meltvedt
All rights reserved.

Editing, Book & Cover Design: Shawn Aveningo Sanders
Cover Photo: Xinyi Song
Author photo: Richard Schmidt

No part of this book may be reproduced in any manner
whatsoever without permission from the author, except
in the case of brief quotations embodied in critical essays,
reviews and articles.

ISBN: 978-1-948461-76-4
Printed in the United States of America.
Wholesale Distribution via Ingram.

Published by The Poetry Box®, 2021
Portland, Oregon
ThePoetryBox.com

*To my mother Beverly Meltvedt
who helped me find voice and whose words
and love I miss every day.*

Contents

Digging	7
Midwest to California Girl	9
Wolf Moon	11
My Father and the Cutting Board	12
Rain as Story	14
1959	15
Why I Am Here (Or, Give Her the Gift of a Patio Table)	17
Unopened	19
Fruit Picking the Morning After	21
Taking the Train to Fresno (Spring 2017)	22
This Is When We Learn to Tingle	23
The J's	26
The Big Dipper	27
Doctor's Office	28
Missing	29
Derby Day	30
Wild Love	32
Reading Ourselves	34
Building a Woman	35
The MRI	37
Mortality	39
Acknowledgments	41
Praise for *Building a Woman*	43
About the Author	45

Digging

In dirt, we didn't grow things,
but we dug, chucked earth
made swirled roads for toy trucks,
took out plastic zebras and gazelles,
poured faucet water
down mounds of clay.
Our own waterfalls
made us yearn for Africa,
just Mary Kay and me,
made us yearn for wildness and purpose,
for saving real things:
a thundered hoof,
the grace of fur flying,
fresh dew on Kilimanjaro.

We found everything in dirt.
What better part of little girl-dom
than to squish the hell out of sugar
and spice and fall half naked
into the open arms of your own backyard?
We were blonde hair spinning,
faces to heavens,
letting loose the sister circle,
inhaling
gasping.
Watch the butterfly swirl,
hear the dragonfly's wing.
Drown out the nighttime voices,
release hands from ears,
find the banquet of reprieve.
Winter still stormed inside the house,
but fog had lifted on the breezeway,
blue blinded the sky,
sparrows spied the shadows,
and mud held court for tiny hands.

Because we knew, as clear as sky,
as painful as the bee sting—
that dirt receives us,
holds up tiny backbones,
lets loose wavy hair.

And so we dug
past worms and twigs,
waved arms to China
till the earth was red, lovely, loosened,
till we became cells before conception,
daughter atoms absorbed,
and fell into the earth
hoping to materialize
past the honey and the spice
as lovely bones that run and race,
as widened mouths that speak up,
as women who, one day,
would become
more than dirt.

Midwest to California Girl

I'm from Iowa plains and
Cecil's café, the tastes of
starched plain donuts, deviled eggs,
and beer-drenched onion rings.

I am the small world of four sisters spinning
on central valley grasses, falling back,
watching hot skies layered
with possibilities.

I am the sound of sprinklers on scorched July days
spraying blessed coolness onto
tanned backs and tangled hair,
of little girls dressed in orange-flowered
swimsuits and shrieking smiles.

I am born of the generation of mothers
who drove in avocado-colored station wagons,
cigarettes drooping out of cherry red mouths,
babies strapped, not in car seats,
but on the laps of sisters
already crowded with sweaty Cokes
and folds of Archie comic books.

I'm from the high school halls of Silence
the voices of anorexic bodies and the secrets
of screaming parents stuffed into lockers
painted with peace signs and psychedelic colors.

I'm from the songs that spoke of making love
not war and from the eyes of young men
that frightened me and lured me all at once.

I am my mother's voice singing
"As Time Goes By" in pink bathrooms
and lime green kitchens.

I'm from the generation
of my father's voice
who spoke of dropping
bombs in Belgium from a P-47
named Mary Ann on late night evenings
when he drank too much vodka
and when he was reminded that
his only son and four daughters
would start to forget
where he was from.

Wolf Moon

On the night of the wolf moon, I dreamt about
dead baby dolls. The ones my sisters and I
decapitated as kids, pulling off their heads
and arms and throwing them at each other
because we were bored and hated the idea
of being a mother one day.

So we mutilated dolls and buried them
in the yard where our dogs once dug up limbs,
chewed the last of plastic skin, and we pretended
they were wolves feeding on leftovers from nasty grownups
one village down.

And now years later, I dream of those dolls,
some with one eye or no hair, dirt caked in their mouths
or belly buttons reminding me of wildness and sister packs
and what we did before we were tamed.

My Father and the Cutting Board

The first time you told
the turkey story I learned
about revenge.

You rolled up your
sleeve and
showed us the scar
saying
*right here right here
eight stiches.*

When it happened
you were only three
years old, no match
for two-foot-tall birds.

You told it again and
again every Thanksgiving,
sharpening the
silver knives, my sisters
and me salivating,
our brother waiting his turn.

Our mother never listened
when you made the first
cut. Up since 5 a.m. she was
still shutting down ovens
wiping things clean
not showing
not ever
her own ancient scars.

I would wonder later
what stories you would tell
if you'd never strayed into
that poultry yard
on a hot Iowa day
and found the world cruel

and later learned that
fighting and carving were
such noble deeds.

So by the tenth or eleventh time
you told the turkey story,
sometimes we rooted
for you, sometimes for
the two-foot-tall bird.

Rain as Story

When I was a child
I drank the rain
April mornings
my sister and I
mouths open like baby birds
feeling wicked and wild.
We flung out arms
twirled on wet grass
feet freezing
hair sopping, slapping cheeks.
But the tulip tree
never looked so pink
against the storm clouds
or our mother
so pleased
watching, behind pelted glass
her daughters
the globe spinners
before we would slow ourselves
fret over thunderstorms and ruined looks
before we would hurry
off the lawn
pull tight the rain jackets
and let the world spin us
before we would begin
to hate ourselves and hate
the taste of rain.

1959

Barbie doll and the Pill
were born the same year,
and I can't help but picture not
Malibu Barbie or Business Barbie,
but Clinic Patient Barbie in the
Planned Parenthood waiting room
curved legs crossed nervously,
pink toes jutting upward while
outside Ken doll leans on the toy red
convertible smoking candy cigarettes,
not hearing when his girlfriend's name
is called and Barbie keeps repeating
It's just Barbie until realizing *Oh, shit,
it's Doll* for the blank space of last name
on the medical history form.

On the scale Barbie weighs .0507 pounds,
and the clinic workers all sigh and say,
"Wow, how do you do it?" They find
a paper gown "that opens in the back,"
and Clinic Barbie meets Gyno Barbie,
who is broad-chested and keeps rubber
gloves in her pocket and says,
"Scoot down, honey; just relax,"
and while Barbie's legs flex in stirrups,
the doctor gasps. Seems Mattel forgot
an opening or two.

But I would be proud of Clinic Barbie
who may be fake in looks, plastic in body,
but if she's gonna mess with Ken, at least
she's not gonna end up being Teenage Mom Barbie.
The Toy Store just needs to stock
the right accessories: tiny pink pill
packets, a plastic speculum, a penis for
Ken. Then Clinic Patient Barbie becomes
the gift we really want for a daughter or

niece as we imagine the TV ads, hear
the jingles between Saturday morning cartoons:

Clinic Barbie combed her hair
Waiting pretty in a clinic chair.
The days were gone of teddy bears;
Our little Barbie had grown-up cares.
But she was smart and Ken was cute,
Though both had missing birthday suits.
We like to think before the deed,
Barb told Ken, "Let's wait to breed."
The downtown clinic was safe and free.
Barb filled out forms and Ken agreed
To get some pills and condoms, too.
Clinic Barbie is responsible—
Are you?

Why I Am Here
(Or, Give Her the Gift of a Patio Table)

I'm here because my mother was not schooled in the art
of her own body, because even married ten years
to a gynecologist
who should have known better, they managed to slip—
let the diaphragm slide from the cervical door—
and my father's fish swam in, caught the egg of my mother's
stern shoulders, but not her blue eyes, and nine months later
a third daughter, fourth unplanned pregnancy, was born.

I'm here because on a brilliant fall day in 1925
when the leaves dripped red and butterscotch, and my mother
(third daughter, fifth unplanned pregnancy)
slid down her own mother's aching slide, my grandfather bought
a new car to ease the pain of the midwife's declaration: *It's a girl!*
He held the steel steering wheel of a blue Ford down thirty miles
of autumn roads before he held the gentle weight—the glory—
of his newborn baby girl, fifth unplanned pregnancy.

I'm here because the day before Mother's Day, before the rush
of roses and rhymes, of past due declarations, a radio announcer
tells me to *Give her the gift of a patio table.* And I laugh because
she wouldn't have wanted pearls or diamonds, but also not plastic
and impermanency. She would have wanted what men want: golf
clubs, recognition, applause. To change the story my grandfather
told in chuckles round the Johnson family reunion, as we sat
stuffed with nostalgia and chips and Midwestern ham
on the frayed fabric of patio chairs and chaise lounges.
I am here because the same radio blast reminds me
that my mother was born in Iowa, where only a car,
not a killing, replaces the shame of not siring another son.

I'm here because my mother at age twenty-six threw away her
stage voice, gave full reins to Judy and Marilyn and Lena,
sold her golf clubs, her slinky red dresses and high-heeled shoes,
let go of dreams to sing on Broadway or win the PGA, who

exchanged fame for the most gorgeous birthday songs sung
to five unplanned children.

And when my father's fish found my mother's egg and
burrowed in like there was no tomorrow—in that mitotic dance,
that fish gave me the brown-eyed *X* but it didn't catch the egg
of long legs and Broadway voices. Instead it caught the egg that
would speak up in ink, not song—the *X* stamped on the hardy
crust of a midwestern fight.
I'm here because the daughter DNA spread like
wildfire on autumn leaves and torched traditions.

Because there was my mother in front of a
thousand mothers who didn't stand high-heeled
on any stage, who didn't clasp diplomas or
turn golf pro, but who felt the diaphragm slip
and pushed out sons and daughters—
who pushed out life for both the wanted
and the other sex.

Unopened

We used to count presents,
my sisters and me, but not
with our brother, who couldn't be bothered
to lower himself onto carpet and
rattle a package because he was the
oldest and got what he wanted.
But the four of us girls crawled under
branches and counted them all—
23, 24, now 52—gifts that gleamed
like promises, giving us grins,
giving us worth.

We made lists for days,
the four of us girls, while
our brother made paper airplanes
and ships, small model cars,
things put together with glue
things put together without
clumsy little girl thumbs.
Ours were girl lists,
hoping for Barbies, pink jackets,
the jangle of bracelets that would
circle our wrists,
things that were shiny,
things we thought we should have.

On Christmas morning, the four of
us girls rose, tangle-haired before dawn,
and we drooled and we waited
for our older brother to rise,
to give us permission to begin.
We sipped orange juice and waited,
listened for the crack of his door, counted again
the silver bows and plaid packages.
And when his ten- or twelve- or
fourteen-year-old feet emerged down
the hall, we tore! We shredded! We
shrieked! We said *look at this* to each

other, to our mother or father, but most
of all to our brother, screaming inside,
look at me! look at me!
Your sister, your very best
unopened gift.

Fruit Picking the Morning After

I first glimpsed *almost truth* in the San Joaquin fields where my mother took us cantaloupe picking and we ate the fruit inside our car on paper towels and I watched my mother's face return like sunrise from a cloudy night. Her lipstick gone, there was bareness and beauty and juice and I would kiss the dots of seeds off her chin and think how gorgeous mothers can be when they ripen, when their hands on knives say, *take this, eat this*, as we devoured flesh and sugar and almost forgot how much we were starving as we wiped away a million kinds of truth.

Taking the Train Home to Fresno
(Spring 2017)

We are flying by treetops
as high as the night train.
Long ago, I would have wanted
to touch their heavens, but
when I tried to jump to
reach the sky, the branches
were as slick and thick as
my father's oiled arms
and my feet heavy and dirty
and the ground reached up and
grabbed me
my father in their claws
my mother in their roots
and I knew
it was impossible
to fly

This is When We Learn to Tingle

This is when we learn to tingle.
Not as babies, even if we are not spanked,
even if aunts, older sisters and grandparents will not let us fall,
will cup us to their full or sunken chests
and hold our diapered butts
and blow wind into our rosebud mouths.
But it is before the boy-kiss-in-the-closet or the circle of knee on
middle school bleachers that peel in the afternoon sun.
It is between the cuddle and the grasp,
between the pinched cheek and the first wide open cut.
We learn to tingle with the girlfriends.

Yellow and blue baby doll pajamas cover
the hint, the slightest wave of curves to come.
We sit cross-legged, long-legged
brown shins still smooth
with soft blonde hairs that have not yet
seen sharpness.
We sit against each other in late night living rooms
on Snoopy sleeping bags
popcorn stuck between teeth
our sex wedged between the butter-smeared bowl
between our thighs and the deep canyon of
what we do not know… yet.

And we giggle, and we clamor,
for the pink polish, the foot rub,
and sometimes the simplest stroke of
stubby fingers down bony backs
"Is it an L?"
"Yes"
Letters materialize across
trapezius and rhomboid muscles
as we guess and melt,
guess and melt.
"Is it an O?"
"Yes"

"A T?" (NO!)
And we continue to guess wrong
because we cannot stand
for the stopping of the shiver

until a rib is jammed and we remember to say
"Is it a V?"
"Yes!"
"An E?"
"Yes!"

And LOVE becomes visible on the backs of
all of us growing up and almost away.

But it is not just the polish or the hands,
but it is the brush we want.
"Do me!"
"Do me!"
And before we know it,
scalps come alive.
Not like our mother's strokes that pulled
like thick, knotted ropes between her ship
and our shores,
but with the girlfriends in 5th, 6th, 7th grade.
The undone ponytail becomes the best catch
in the gentle hands of Jackie or Janet or Lisa or Jill
and scalps tingle.

And for the first time
you know sex
in the way the first boyfriend won't or
the magazines will not advertise
and in a way you cannot name,
until much later the boy or the man draws words
upon your back and out your mouth
and something else emerges,
something else that multiplies the electricity
that runs far beyond the muscles in your back.

Until years later
you lean against crisp sheets
and brush your mother's white hair, thin
as a newborn's, in a sterile bed
on the 4th floor, and you are careful
not to tug the rope too tight, to fight the knots,
even though the break is coming,
because the old words are emerging.
And your ring finger draws L and O and V and E
across the inside of her blue-veined wrist
and, once again, everything, from toe to scalp,
begins to tingle.

The J's

Most of my friends' names begin with J
one Jill
two Jannas
a Janet, a Jan, a Jodi, a Julie
half a dozen Jennifers
one Jackie and Jean
half a June
because we don't talk anymore
but June was the first that kindergarten day
when we looked each other over
and discovered a new kind of love.

And I claim these J's
because my middle name is Jean
and I wanted it to be my first
because J names are beautiful
and who wouldn't want to be
a carve of constellation that
lights up your sky or the
driver on earth
speeding up to save you?

The Big Dipper

My cat drops kibble in the shape of constellations.
In our kitchen you need to be careful not to step on crunchy stars.
In his first life of nine, before we claimed him,
someone kicked our cat in the jaw and sent him flying.
The foster cat for free became the $900 aftermath
of annual teeth cleaning and tooth extraction.

To eat, he starts with a mouthful of dry food
then loses half the battle.

But in violence, stars were born.

And a ten-pound pack of fur and bone and very few teeth
somehow gives me hope in a world of angry boots,
gives me hope when I read about the darkest corners of humans
carrying torches that never give light.

And I realize that even the smallest of critters can survive
hatred and even make me laugh when I look down
and see the sky on the most ordinary of earthly floors.

Doctor's Office

I grew up in the land of gynecology—
women waiting.
There is the push of heavy doors
into my father's practice.
We are dropped into the back room like shopping bags
to wait with Highlights magazines and obstetrical manuals,
eating Saltine crackers and drinking 7 Up.
We play with the silliness of plastic wombs,
finger fallopian tubes,
think of drawing fat smiles
on the moose-head likeness of uterine anatomy charts.

In later years, we work in his office
in the kingdom of white coats—
women waiting.
Words like mittleschmertz, yeast infections,
and salpingoopherectomy
fall easily off our tongues.
We laugh at the woman on the other side of the phone
who claims her vibrator makes her pee.
And we look down, solemn-eyed, when
the sound of the Doppler goes silent
against the bulge of a belly
that ripened once, then shriveled.

Years later, I make my own appointments
in towns far from my father's reign.
And when my name is called,
I squeeze polite-lipped through a room of
sausage legs and swollen bodies
of women giving so much more of themselves away.

Years later, I kill time
lying against paper sheets,
bite my own tongue when the doctor
reaches for something soft beneath my soul,
learn to scoot down and shut up
to stare up at ceilings   waiting.

Missing

In a manila bed
it rests—
on the peeling kitchen shelf
wedged on the ledge
we access by the tallest of our tiptoes
on sturdy, ugly chairs.

Here, she holds up Terminology:
endometrium, spontaneous abortion, blighted zygote.

Out of reach
like the leftover lamb
held high on a plate,
far from the begging dog
so tall on its hind legs,
but not tall enough
to reach the shelf.

Derby Day

You saw us choose,
pick our favorites,
point our bitten nails
sealed in plastic
against the tiny print
of the sports section on that
Kentucky Derby Day—
#7, #12 with names like Lucky George,
Galloping Go Lightly or
Sparks Will Fly.

You heard us roar—
our masks pulled down for
full-throttle screams,
as if we were spectators in the stands
wearing flaming hats,
throwing rose petals to the
sweaty backs of bays and grays.

And, we—
the ones you've birthed and
fallen for,
the ones you've let out of the gate,
your son and daughters
who brought you the
paper, the sports section you loved,
the wilted roses dying on the sill—
we almost never noticed
how you opted out,
refused the bets, refused to look.
Instead you lay back, IV drip
mind wide open.

And you heard the cheer—
the collective cry for the horse
that came from far behind
some 9 ½ lengths—
towards glory, towards rest.

And, I, too, closed my eyes
let tissues fall like confetti
in room 408, listening
to the thunder of hearts bursting,
and wanting, deep down inside
to slow the last lap
of that famous race.

Wild Love

As girls,
we wanted wildness,
tried to find it on our
fathers' backs in swimming
pools in July when the sun
was still wanted
when our legs were still small and dark,
crossed against our Dad's sunburned chest,
and we shouted, "Throw me! Throw me!"
his hands reaching back and we
flew into the deep end, laughing
because we wanted flight, screaming
because we needed wildness.

In fall, we settled for
swing sets after school
pumping legs before our
thighs became liabilities,
and then we found that first
spread across a pony's sloped back
at the Fresno county fair,
flight as slow as turtles,
her mane like straw, our grins alive,
and then we found the second one
at your best friend's grandfather's ranch,
San Joaquin Valley, 105 degrees,
his hands cupped, your sneaker
lifted in trust and then
you mount the black one,

and your thighs
    before they shuddered in love
    before they struggled into last year's jeans or
      this year's skirt
    before you saw them in fitting room mirrors
      and gasped at flesh
    before hate
your thighs straddled the black one,

and wildness whipped
through fat and femur
through blood and bone,

and you laughed
because you fell in love with horses,
and you screamed
because it was the time
when you loved yourself.

Reading Ourselves

We wanted to believe we were poetry in motion
ready to be read that summer
like Dickinson's *wild nights*.
We were poetry with painted eyes,
stanzas shaking silver,
our arms waving laughter
tank tops moving like Neruda's
pen across a mountain top.

We drank the white and the red,
the ones boys bought us
as we metered up and down the bar
with no ID, just an opening
line that asked *please like me*,
our smiles a simile like the shyness
of a child pleading at your knee.
The boys bought us the white and
the red. We didn't question being
dizzy on the dance floor—
we thought we were weak-hearted
we hoped we were worth the recitation
of *damn, girl, you look good tonight*.

I like to think nothing awful really happened—
too many girlfriends standing with claws ready.
I like to think we were cupped in men's hands,
understood between difficult lines,
even if it took years to find our way to
reading ourselves.

Building a Woman

Give her the double X without the reason Y
because Adam is supposed to ask the questions.

Start with Daddy's girl.
Call her Sweetheart, Princess, Little Lady
but most of all Beautiful. Paint her toes pink
so she can find them in the darkness.
Pierce her ears with pearls that tilt her head
to listen when the Ys talk about themselves.
Blow into her mouth the stale butter of apology
and fatten her bell with swollen mistakes.

Make her good at learning, but quiet her for asking Y.
Pen her eyes to look down, her legs to cross.
Fill her tendons with roses, her muscles with iron
so she can run fast—but not so fast she passes all the Ys.
Make her mind grateful for the smallest of wages, her bones
to bend and picked up what we've all dropped a thousand times.

Fashion her hips into the slope of hills where children
will settle in cool shade and grabbed by the hands of Ys
to whirl her on the dance floor. Make those hips to be noticed.
Craft her thighs out of rising Pillsbury dough, soft enough to make
her hate them at fourteen so she does not fill up on her own
    sweetness.

Style her hair to change like weather, prone to humidity and
    dryness.
Make her drool over promises of long and silky.

Build a woman with a nest the size of her fist that will rise monthly
and spill secrets and teardrops, preparing
to make lots of Xs and Ys
because the Ys made her believe that the nest is herself.

Don't forget to carve "Miss" across her chest in tiny pink skin.
And when one of the Ys asks for her hand, get out the knife,
X out "Miss," and carve in "taken" so she can buy

drugstore mugs with her new title in gold and stand in line
at the DMV because she has taken on a new name.

Build her for standing in long lines, make sure she says,
"X-cuse me,"
though she and other Xs get bumped from behind.

X-cept sometimes the blueprint will fade,
become pink print or plaid. She will not follow directions.
A double X will start asking Y, will pick up the tools
and rearrange her own limbs. She will fill up her bones,
open her chest, leaving only the M and the S,
and X out what never belonged.

The MRI

The technician told me
he knew
as soon as I put my hand up
and grabbed metal,
before I yelled, "Stop!"
before I cried, "I can't do it!"
He said he gets two or three just like me every day.
Then added,
maybe another time.
Then *it's okay.*

When I return to the waiting room
my husband looks up and says,
"So soon?"
and my tears start again
so he holds me
lets me unfold
hears me sob-saying,
"The Valium didn't work."

Outside the sky is drizzling.
In the parking garage my husband
has trouble figuring out the payment machine.
The attendant is patient:
No, like this.
No problem.
There are three or four an hour just like
him every day.

We pull out of darkness,
the parking garage lever lifts,
a mother opens blinds,
the child unlocks her bedroom door.

We pull out of darkness
because the doctor judged, but
the technician was kind.

Because somebody says,
*No worries, we see you.
We see three or four or more*
just like you every day.
Just like you.

Mortality

Overheard yesterday
my students debating
the best age to die

Diana said sixty
Fabian nodded
Lenore thought fifty-two
Adrian agreed

I listen
thinking of their "terms"
my own clock coming past
their keys to destiny
as if endings were a choice

them declining the small slice of cherry pie
after the briefest of meals
feeling so full at eighteen

and me still hungry
watching them leave
as I lock the classroom door

Acknowledgments

I would like to thank the editors of the following publications for publishing my work in previous anthologies and literary journals:

"Digging" (as "What We Are Made Of") – *Tule Review* (Sacramento Poetry Center, February 2012)

"My Father and the Cutting Board" – *Sacramento Voices* (Cold River Press, Sept 2015)

"Rain as Story" – *Soul of the Narrator* (Team Haag Anthology, Vol. IX, November 2018)

"1959" – *The Poeming Pigeon: Pop Culture* (The Poetry Box, 2020)

"Why I Am Here" – *Tule Review* (Sacramento Poetry Center, Fall 2012)

"This is When We Learn to Tingle" – *Soul of the Narrator* (Team Haag Anthology, Vol. IV, June 2013)

"Big Dipper" – *Soul of the Narrator* (Team Haag Anthology, Vol. VIII, November 2017)

"Doctor's Office" – *Sussurus: The Sacramento City College Literary Journal* (2010)

"Missing" – *Tule Review* (Sacramento Poetry Center, February 2012)

"Derby Day" – *Sussurus: The Sacramento City College Literary Journal* (2011)

Thank you to Shawn Aveningo Sanders and the staff at The Poetry Box for publishing my work in previous anthologies and for publishing my very first book of poetry. I am also extremely grateful to the Sacramento writing community, especially my fellow writers in Team Haag's Saturday morning writing group. Their encouragement, laughter, and talent laid the foundation for almost all of these poems. A special thanks to our leader, Jan Haag, who spent so much time and energy in helping me edit and revise my poetry. Jan's love and support for my work has kept me going when my pen (and insecurity) often failed me. Also, thanks to Richard Schmidt who took my photo for this book, one of the few photos I have ever liked of myself.

I especially want to thank the women in my life who contributed to my experiences and perceptions that made these poems come alive. My sisters (and sister-out law), nieces, friends in Sacramento, and especially my life-long friends from Fresno. I thank you all for loving me and saving me.

And, of course, I am forever grateful to my husband, Rick Kushman, who embraces feminism, gives me writing prompts, endures hearing my first draft of poems, loves me on days I find difficult to love myself, and who can hang with the best of my women friends.

Praise for Building a Woman

Building a Woman is composed of poems that showcase Deborah Meltvedt's unique voice in which she delves into her personal history and offers it like a mirror, exposed and shining, to readers. She draws upon childhood's wishes, adolescence with all its loves and losses, and womanhood's strengths and vulnerabilities. Her words ring out like bells and call to us like a friend, urging us to come visit; stay a while; enjoy.

—Anara Guard, author of *Hand on My Heart*

Building a Woman presents a series of candid poems that tell Deborah Meltvedt's story of girl-dom, of growing up one of four daughters in California's central valley, struggling to make sense of family discord, budding sexuality and feminism. She accomplishes this with arresting images and precise language that chronicles a woman's journey to self-acceptance and love, she writes, that "becomes visible on the backs of/ all of us growing up and almost away." The poems not only illustrate Meltvedt's life experiences but also offer unflinching glimpses into the universal challenges and joys of what it is to be female moving from one millennium to another.

—Jan Haag, author of *Companion Spirit*

Deborah Meltvedt weaves words into magic carpets that transport the reader through imagery, memory, and experience—pulling threads from pain, grief, shame, triumph and joy. Her writing takes my breath and rearranges me—in all of the best ways.

—Jodi Angel, author of *You Only Get Letters from Jail* and *The History of Vegas*

About the Author

Deborah Meltvedt is a high school teacher who loves to blend medical science and art in both the classroom and in her own writing. Deborah grew up in the suburbs and fields of the San Joaquin Valley whose landscapes and culture form a backbone to her poetry. As a doctor's daughter and feminist, she feels strongly about women's health and reproductive rights and respecting the traditional and non-traditional paths women take in their lives.

Her poems and stories have been published in the *American River Literary Review, Susurrus, Under the Gum Tree, Tule Review, The Poeming Pigeon,* and the Creative Non-Fiction Anthology *What I Didn't Know: True Stories of Becoming a Teacher.*

Deborah lives in Sacramento with her funny and supportive husband, Rick Kushman, and their cat, Anchovy Jack, who in his former life used to be a pirate.

About The Poetry Box®

The Poetry Box® is a boutique publishing company in Portland, Oregon, who provides a platform for both established and emerging poets to share their words with the world through beautiful printed books and chapbooks.

Feel free to visit the online bookstore (thePoetryBox.com), where you'll find more titles including:

Nothing More to Lose by Carolyn Martin

Notes from a Caregiver by Meg Lindsay

Like the O in Hope by Jeanne Julian

A Shape of Sky by Cathy Cain

The Very Rich Hours by Gregory Loselle

Just the Girls by Pamela R. Anderson-Bartholet

Between States of Matter by Sherry Rind

The Kingdom of Birds by Joan Colby

Off Coldwater Canyon by C.W. Emerson

Excoriation by Rebecca Smolen

What She Was Wearing by Shawn Aveningo Sanders

My Mother Never Died Before by Marcia B. Loughran

Mouth Quill by Kaja Weeks

and more . . .

www.ingramcontent.com/pod-product-compliance
Lightning Source LLC
LaVergne TN
LVHW040203080526
838202LV00042B/3292